WOMEN OF SPORTS

THE BEST OF THE BEST
in
Soccer

BY
RACHEL RUTLEDGE

THE MILLBROOK PRESS
BROOKFIELD, CONNECTICUT

Produced by
CRONOPIO PUBLISHING
John Sammis, President
and
TEAM STEWART, INC.

Series Design and Electronic Page Makeup by
JAFFE ENTERPRISES
Ron Jaffe

Researched and Edited by Mark Stewart and Michael Kennedy

Special thanks to Joe Provey and *SOCCER JR.* Magazine

All photos courtesy AP/WIDE WORLD PHOTOS, INC. except the following:

ROB TRINGALI/SPORTS CHROME:
Cover (Mia Hamm, Canada vs. USA, 1997)

SIDELINE SPORTS PHOTOGRAPHY, MICHAEL STAHLSCHMIDT
Pages 13, 19, 25, 28, 34, 40, 46, 49, 52, 60

PHIL STEPHENS PHOTOGRAPHY
Pages 2, 14, 22, 38, 42, 44, 50, 55, 56, 58

THE NATIONAL SOCCER HALL OF FAME, ONEONTA, NY—Pages 6, 8

Printed in the United States of America

Published by
The Millbrook Press, Inc.
2 Old New Milford Road
Brookfield, Connecticut   06804

http://www.millbrookpress.com

Library of Congress Cataloging-in-Publication Data
Rutledge, Rachel.
   The best of the best in soccer/ by Rachel Rutledge.
   p.   cm.   — (Women of Sports)
   Includes index.
   Summary; Discusses the past and future of women's soccer and presents biographies of eight
of the sport's most famous players: Michelle Akers, Joy Fawcett, Julie Foudy, Mia Hamm,
Kristine Lilly, Shannon MacMillan, Carla Overbeck, and Briana Scurry.
   ISBN 0-7613-1907-7 (lib. bdg.).—ISBN 0-7613-1392-3 (pbk.)
   1. Women Soccer players—Biography—Juvenile literature. 2. Soccer for women—Juvenile
literature. [1. Soccer players. 2. Women—Biography. 3. Soccer for women.]
I. Title.   II. Series: Best of the best in soccer.
GV944.9.A1R88 1998
796.334'082'0922
[B]—DC21
                                                                                          98-25635
                                                                                              CIP
                                                                                              AC

pbk: 10 9 8 7 6 5 4 3 2 1
lib: 10 9 8 7 6 5 4 3 2 1

CONTENTS

In the Beginning

Although soccer is one of the world's oldest sports, women's soccer is one of the newest. For a good part of the last century, females have been dissuaded, discouraged and sometimes even banned from playing the game, which existed on the fringes of the mainstream sports scene. Soccer is fast, rough and strenuous—and almost always played in shorts—so until relatively recent times, it was considered totally inappropriate by those who purported to understand the "limits" of the female mind and body.

The 1970s saw the first real opportunities for girls to play organized soccer, both in this country and overseas. Prior to that, they had to play in leagues for boys. During the 1980s, there was an explosion of both girls' and mixed-sex youth leagues, and by the early 1990s women's soccer was well-established in high schools and colleges in North America, Latin America, the Pacific Rim and Europe. The sad part of this story is that it took so long. The happy part—for the United States and the women's game, in general—is that everyone started at the same time and on equal footing. In other words, there was instant parity. That had not been the case in men's soccer, where British teams ruled the field for 75 years before everyone else caught up.

For centuries, the sport had thrived in England under the name of "football," although it bore scant resemblance to today's game. Until the mid-1800s, in fact, a typical football match amounted to no more than a thinly veiled version of mob violence. It featured pushing, shoving, kicking, biting and punching, and the exhausted participants generally quit after a single goal had been scored or someone had been mortally wounded. These games were not played in open fields, but right through the middle of cities and villages. "Teams" of 50 or more men barreled down the muddy streets trying to overwhelm each other.

At various times, royal decrees were issued banning the sport. In fact, the first woman whose name was associated with soccer was Queen Elizabeth I, who in 1572 outlawed football in London after reading a horrifying report that claimed players' "necks are broken, sometimes their backs or legs, sometimes their noses gush out blood, and sometimes their eyes are put out." The temptation to butt heads and blow off a little steam was simply too tempting, however, and the game lived on. By the early 1600s football was legal again, and was even starting to gain support in some respectable circles. Still, with such a sullied reputation, it is small wonder that football was deemed unfit for ladies.

In the latter stages of the 18th century, football—in a far more organized (and far less lethal) form—began to undergo a facelift. The people who ran England's private schools changed their minds about the merits of physical education, and football seemed an ideal game for their students. It was one of the few sports that a group of boys could play at the same time, and it required a minimal amount of equipment. Within 50 years, the upper class had taken the game from the lower class, polished it up a bit, and made it their own.

When soccer first came to the U.S., it was still an extremely rough game.

When these boys completed their education and entered the business world, they maintained their school and professional affiliations by forming social clubs. One of the many activities of these clubs was football. Because the rules of the game had differed from school to school, each club played a slightly different version. In order to play against one another, the clubs had to come to an agreement on a standard set of rules.

This presented a problem. Football was still in its formative stages. Many preferred the version which allowed a player to pick up the ball and run with it until he was tackled. Indeed, for several decades, there were two types of football: the rugby-like "carrying" game and the more soccer-like "kicking" or "dribbling" game.

In 1848, the first comprehensive set of rules for modern soccer was published by J.C. Thring of Cambridge University. The sport split once and for all from rugby in 1863, when several clubs met to form England's Football Association, which outlawed tackling another player, and picking the ball up while it was in play. From that time on, the sport was called "Association Football," whereas its rival was called "Rugby Football." How did the name "Soccer" come about? It was the style of the time to shorten names by taking a word's first syllable and adding "er" to it. Therefore, Rugby Football became "Rugger." That did not really work for Association Football (it is highly doubtful anyone would have played a game called "Asser"), so players chose the "soc" in the middle of "Association" and came up with "Soccer."

The first women's clubs began forming in the 1890s around London. One team in particular, from Preston, gained quite a reputation, and became famous throughout the empire. In 1902 the Preston club boarded a steamship to the United States for a series of exhibition matches against the women's clubs forming in the New Jersey-New York-Boston area, which at the time was the center of America's "soccer universe." That same year, England's Football Association, which claimed to govern all soccer clubs, refused admission to women's teams. The organization

The undefeated British women's international team of 1920-21. Despite a surge in participation during the 1920s, the popularity of women's soccer—both in Europe and the U.S.—ebbed during the 1930s and '40s.

stubbornly upheld its decision, even as women's soccer continued to develop a fairly strong international following. In 1920, for instance, a crowd of more than 10,000 showed up to watch a game between England and France.

Although women's soccer was encouraged by soccer's worldwide governing body, FIFA (Federation Internationale de Football Association), in the four decades that followed, women's soccer failed to gain much ground. Chauvinistic attitudes toward women and sports still prevailed in most countries, and there was not much interest in the women's game from the late 1920s to the mid 1950s, when the world was busy dealing

A scramble for the ball during the 1957 European Ladies Soccer Championship between Great Britain and West Germany. By the late-'50s, women's soccer was beginning to gain some of the ground it had lost.

with a global economic depression, a world war and a long and complicated recovery period. By the 1960s, however, the winds of change were beginning to blow.

In 1968, the Football Association finally recognized women's soccer. In the United States, a legal battle culminating in the passage of the Education Act of 1972 also helped soccer immensely. Title IX of that act stated that no one could be excluded from participation in any educational program or activity on the basis of sex. Although not aimed specifically at college sports, it did wonders for women's athletics. It was at this point that women's soccer started to receive funding at a handful of colleges. Though it would be a while before soccer scholarships and big traveling and equipment budgets would be available, the women's game was beginning to take root in America.

In 1981, the NCAA (National Collegiate Athletic Association) announced it would sanction the first women's national championship tournament. This touched off a burst of interest on college campuses around the United States. For so long, women's soccer had been relegated to intramural- or club-sport status. Now it would be a part of varsity athletic programs. By the mid-1980s, there were 200 women's teams in college soccer, and by the end of the '80s, the first wave of graduates went out into the world and formed the backbone of several strong women's amateur leagues. The dominant program in college soccer was the University of North Carolina, which won the first NCAA tournament in 1982, and also ran off a string of nine national championships between 1986 and 1994, under the reign of coach Anson Dorrance.

In 1991, FIFA staged the first Women's World Championship in China, modeled after the men's World Cup. The United States national team surprised the experts by winning the tournament. Both the winner

The first U.S. women's intercollegiate soccer tournament, held in 1975, was won by the University of Vermont. Here, Vermont's Becky Hitchcock and Cathy Cobb of the Emma Willard School battle for the ball.

and venue were very significant. China's entry into FIFA had swelled the organization's ranks and increased its influence in Asia, where soccer was booming. The U.S., meanwhile, could claim around half of the world's soccer-playing women.

In 1993, it was announced that women's soccer would be added as a medal event to the 1996 Olympics in Atlanta. This put another big charge into the game, both abroad and in the United States, where the number of varsity college programs totaled nearly 400. There is nothing more appealing to an athlete than winning an Olympic medal, and suddenly the best college players had a shot at that dream.

More progress followed. The 1991 championship in China evolved into the first official Women's World Cup in 1995. The tournament was held in Sweden (Scandinavia has long been a fertile area for women's soccer) and it was won by the powerhouse team from Norway, which defeated Team USA in the semifinals. In 1996, the Americans avenged that loss during the Olympics, with a dramatic sudden-death goal to defeat Norway in the semifinals. That set up a gold medal showdown with China.

The U.S. national team—led by the players profiled in the following chapters—took the women's game to a new level by defeating the Chinese in front of 76,000 delirious fans. Now these same players find themselves in a situation that is unique in the annals of athletics: They are pioneers, yet they also represent the future of their sport. That is how fast things have happened in women's soccer!

Charismatic stars like Mia Hamm (center) kept women's soccer in the spotlight after the Olympics.

ON HER MIND

"My teammates and I have given something to young female soccer players that we never had as kids—someone to be like."

Michelle Akers

To be a sports pioneer, you must be willing to put up with a lot. You have to be willing to toil in obscurity and you must sacrifice your body. You may have to put up with horrendous conditions, and you can just forget about making any money. Then, if you are really lucky, someone might actually remember you when your playing days are over. Rare are the athletes who have the talent, courage, and perseverance to pick up a sport and carry it on their backs. But then, it takes a special individual to do something like that. In women's soccer, that person is Michelle Akers.

Michelle is the most dynamic scoring threat in the history of the women's game. When she began playing at the age of eight, however, she was a goalie. It drove her crazy not to be in on the action, and when her Police Athletic League team lost, she usually cried. "When you're the goalie you think every loss is your fault," she says.

Michelle worked hard to improve her dribbling and passing skills, and she tried to copy the great Pele, who had just joined the New York Cosmos of the North American Soccer League. She learned how to juggle the ball just as she had seen the Brazilian star do: from her feet to her thighs to her head and back down to her thighs and feet. By the age of 10, Michelle was good enough to play center. Over the next few years she developed a strong and accurate shot, and could head the ball with great precision.

By her sophomore year at Seattle's Shorecrest High School, Michelle was already one of the best players in the country. She was fast, powerful, smart and aggressive, and she only got better with time. In the early 1980s, few colleges had good programs for women. The University of

Michelle is one of the players who "made" women's soccer in the U.S. She plans to be involved with the sport long after she retires.

Michelle and Carla Overbeck (right) put a lot of years' work into winning the gold medal at the 1996 Olympics.

Central Florida, in Orlando, was one of them. Michelle accepted a scholarship from the school and had a brilliant career, earning All-America honors four times and winning the very first women's Hermann Award as the nation's top player.

In 1985, Michelle heard that U.S. Soccer was forming a women's national team. The prospect of competing internationally was very appealing to her. Unlike the American men, who lagged decades behind their peers in Europe and Latin America, the American women had relatively little "catching up" to do. Top-level women's soccer was only about 10 years old, and half of the female soccer players in the world were at colleges and clubs in the United States. Michelle believed Team USA could dominate women's soccer and put the sport on the map in the U.S. She made the team and scored a goal in her second international match.

Michelle soon realized that she possessed some skills that, at that time, were unique to women's soccer. Whereas most goals were scored from 50 feet and in, she could put the ball in the net from twice that distance. She could also handle the ball well enough to create her own shots, meaning that opponents had to double- and triple-team her. This often resulted in one or two of her teammates being unguarded, in which case

Getting Personal

Michelle was born on February 1, 1966...During the 1970s, Michelle thought she might like to play for the NFL's Pittsburgh Steelers, but a teacher told her girls could not play football... In 1988, she attended a clinic conducted by the Dallas Cowboys' kicking coach. She booted several 50-yard field goals and was told that, if she was interested, she had a real shot at being the first woman to play in the NFL...Michelle was named Central Florida's Athlete of the Year in 1989...In 1998, she received the FIFA Order of Merit... In 1999, Michelle scored her 100th career goal...She is the spokesperson for the Chronic Fatigue Immune Disorder Association of America.

Michelle would make a long cross to the open player. When the defense shifted to chase the ball, she would steam toward the goal for a return pass. Needless to say, she created a lot of havoc—especially toward the end of a game, when players get tired and lose a half-step.

The team got steadily better as more top college players joined, and in 1991 Michelle and company reached the finals of FIFA's first Women's World Championship. In that game, against the favored Norwegian team, Michelle was a one-woman wrecking crew. She had already scored eight goals during the tournament, and had played her heart out. More than 60,000 fans packed Tianhe Stadium in Guangzhou, China, waiting to see what the American superstar would do with everything on the line. Michelle brought the crowd to its feet time and again, and she scored Team USA's first goal on a wonderful header. With a few minutes left and the score knotted 1-1, Michelle spotted Norway's usually reliable Tina Svensson making a lackadaisical backpass to goalie Reidun Seth. Michelle bolted toward the goal, collected the ball before Seth could get to it and blasted it into the net for the winning score.

Michelle's performance was nothing short of amazing. Just as amazing was the fact that she made it to the world championships at all. Her aggressive playing style had cost her a couple of teeth, caused at least one concussion, and led to no fewer than seven knee operations in six years. But it was all worth it when the team got back home and found the sport

Career Highlights

Year	Team	Achievement
1981–1983	Shorecrest High	H.S. All-American
1984, 1986–1988	Central Florida	First-Team All-American
1987–1988	Central Florida	NCAA Player of the Year
1989	Central Florida	Hermann Award Winner
1990–1991	Team USA	US Soccer Female Athlete of the Year
1991	Team USA	FIFA World Champion
1992	Tyreso	Swedish League Scoring Champion
1996	Team USA	MVP of US Women's Cup
1996	Team USA	Olympic Gold Medalist
1998	Team USA	Goodwill Games Gold Medalist
1999	Team USA	World Cup Champion & All-Star

of women's soccer totally energized. The "icing on the cake" for Michelle was that her all-time hero, Pele, told reporters that he thought she was just fantastic.

In the years that followed, Michelle continued her full soccer schedule. But she often felt woozy during games and uncharacteristically listless off the field. The strange feeling got progressively worse, but Michelle tried to ignore it. Finally, she became delirious during a 1994 match and agreed to go see some specialists. They diagnosed her with a form of Chronic Fatigue Syndrome. Michelle was relieved to know she was actually sick, but the symptoms only worsened from there. "The worst was total debilitation," she says, "just this bone-weary exhaustion...I had migraines that would last for days, and I would lie there and wish I would die."

Michelle had to summon all of the mental strength and discipline she had once devoted to soccer and now apply it to her daily life. Getting out of bed and going to the grocery store was more grueling than any workout she had ever endured. To make matters even worse, her marriage of four years to soccer player Roby Stahl broke up.

In 1996, things began to look brighter for Michelle. She made radical changes to her diet and began to notice she had more energy. Then she began taking electrolyte replacement solution after her workouts and stopped having the searing headaches. Encouraged by this progress,

Michelle made several dramatic lifestyle changes (in other words, she began taking it easy) and decided she had a real shot at playing in the Olympics.

She trained hard and got back into top form just in time for the Olympic Games. By the time Team USA met archrival Norway in the semifinals, Michelle was totally locked in. She erased a 1-0 deficit with a penalty kick, and kept up the pressure until the team scored the tiebreaker in sudden death to advance to the gold-medal final. Michelle's comeback meant a lot to her teammates. Not only was she an inspirational leader, but by helping the team defeat Norway, she ensured that they would all split a quarter-million dollar bonus for reaching the final. For a sport that offers little in the way of monetary compensation, that was huge.

After taking some time off to recover from her 13th knee operation, Michelle returned to Team

Michelle has been darting through defenses since the early 1980s. No one has devised a reliable way to stop her yet.

USA in the fall of 1997 and scored two goals in her first game back. In 1998, she was honored by FIFA for her contributions to soccer, and in 1999, she scored her 100th career goal. Although it will soon be time to hang up her cleats, Michelle says she will never cut her ties to the game. "I'll always be a spokeswoman for women's soccer," she says.

"I wouldn't be happy if I wasn't constantly doing something."

Joy Fawcett

I f a vote were ever held for America's "Ultimate Soccer Mom," Joy Fawcett would win it hands-down. No one has ever managed to intertwine family and soccer as tirelessly and successfully as she has. In fact, it is unlikely that anyone would even be willing to try. Joy has been a big name in the sport since she was anointed the nation's top player more than a decade ago. She has been a respected coach and teacher since taking over the UCLA women's team in 1993. And now she is a mother of two little girls. Of all the players who mounted the winner's stand to receive gold medals at the 1996 Olympics, no one deserved it more than Joy.

Her soccer career began in Huntington Beach, where she established herself as the finest schoolgirl player in Southern California. A talented and tough two-way player, Joy led Edison High to the league championship in each of her four varsity seasons, and earned a scholarship to the University of California at Berkeley. There she shattered the school scoring mark and

No one was happier than Joy when the national team beat China 2-1 to win the gold medal at the 1996 Olympics.

Joy played every minute of every game during the 1996 Olympics. Having her on the field was like having a "second coach." Her heady play helped keep the ball out of Team USA's net.

made All-America three times. As a sophomore in 1987, Joy netted an amazing 23 goals for Cal and played sparkling defense as she led the team to the NCAA semifinals. In 1988, she was named U.S. Soccer's Female Athlete of the Year.

After graduation, Joy set her sight on making a name for herself on the national team. This she did in short order, developing into the world's best "offensive defender." Joy possessed a scorer's mentality, which helped her get inside the heads of the players she had to stop. That mentality also came in handy when play turned the other way, as she often joined the attack. Joy and Carla Overbeck squeezed the life out of opposing offenses in the 1991 Women's World Championships, enabling Team USA to score a surprising victory.

In 1992 and 1993, Joy played for the Ajax club of Manhattan Beach, California, leading that team to the U.S. Amateur National Cup both years. In 1993, Joy also became UCLA's first women's soccer coach, adding yet another feather to her cap. The Bruins fashioned a solid 10-6-1 record in their inaugural season, as Joy managed to whip a young and inexperienced team into shape despite being pregnant with her first child. Katelyn was born the following May.

Getting Personal

Joy was born on February 8, 1968, in Inglewood, California...She learned soccer from her older brother, Eric, who went on to play for the men's national team in the 1980s...When Joy was a high school senior, her brother was a star on the UCLA team that won the NCAA title...As a college sophomore Joy played for the West squad at the U.S. Olympic Festival and led the team to a gold medal...She is still Cal-Berkeley's all-time scoring leader with 55 goals and 23 assists...Joy graduated from college with a degree in physical education...One of Joy's biggest fans is teammate Michelle Akers, who calls her "Wonder Woman"...Joy's girls are named Katelyn and Carli...She led UCLA from mediocrity to the 1997 PAC 10 championship before stepping down in December of that year...Although Joy makes juggling soccer and parenthood look easy, she is the first to admit it is not. "You have to do something every single day, or you lose it," she maintains. "It's hard to keep motivated. I have to drag myself out every day and do something, even if it's by myself."

The energetic young coach just kept plugging along. And under Joy's tutelage, UCLA kept getting better. She taught her players how to defend

Career *Highlights*

Year	Team	Achievement
1985	Edison High	Southern California Soccer MVP
1987–1989	California	First-Team All-American
1988	California	US Soccer Female Athlete of the Year
1991	Team USA	FIFA World Champion
1992–1993	Ajax	US Amateur Champion
1996	Team USA	Olympic Gold Medalist
1997	UCLA	PAC 10 Coach of the Year
1998	Team USA	Goodwill Games Gold Medalist
1998	Team USA	MVP of US Women's Cup
1999	Team USA	World Cup Champion

against every attack imaginable, and dared her scorers to beat her one-on-one. The team improved steadily, winning 11 games in 1994 and 14 in 1995. Incredibly, during this time, Joy also coached a local youth league team!

Needless to say, a lot of people began asking Joy how she did it. She was quick to give credit to her mom and husband, Walter, who pitched in whenever her schedule got impossibly hectic. Still, Joy always felt she could be doing more for her sport. In 1995, she joined the national team in preparation for the '96 Games in Atlanta. Unfortunately, Joy broke her leg, which many observers felt would put an end to her playing career. By the time the team got to Atlanta, however, Joy had made a full recovery. In fact, according to Team USA coach Tony DiCicco, she was the best defender at the tournament. That says a lot, especially when one considers how dominant the team was at both ends of the field.

It did not take an expert to spot Joy's contributions. She was her usual brilliant self, snuffing out scoring chances and then adeptly turning the ball back up the field with her great vision and tremendous speed. During the gold medal game against China, Joy spotted teammate Tiffeny Milbrett and hit her with a perfect pass, which she drilled into the net for the game-winning goal!

Joy took time off from Team USA to have her second child, but continued to coach UCLA through the 1997 season. In 1998, she returned to the national squad, and won MVP honors at the U.S. Women's Cup, scoring the opening goal in the finals against Brazil. Her play during World Cup '99 was a major factor in the U.S. victory, and she plans to be an even bigger contributor at the 2000 Olympics.

Being a top defender means you sometimes have to maneuver your way out of trouble. Joy's dribbling skills rank among the very best at her position.

ON HER MIND

"I can run all day, and I have vision. I can see the whole field and play everywhere. I'm the playmaker."

Julie Foudy

ith success comes responsibility. In fact, the more you achieve in this world, the more weight this world expects you to shoulder. Julie Foudy, co-captain of the women's national soccer team, understands what comes with the territory. She not only accepts and embraces her role as one of the leading figures in women's soccer, she goes at it as if it were a loose ball. Indeed, Julie has meant as much to the team's success—and to the future of soccer—as anyone in the sport.

The first time Julie felt she had a future in soccer was at the age of six. She would kick one of those big red balls around with her classmates in rag-tag recess games, and she got a real charge when she managed to score a goal. Though Julie admits she was not particularly good, she really wanted to sign up for one of the local youth league teams in Mission Viejo, California. "I begged my mom to get me involved," she remembers.

Julie developed quickly thanks to good coaching and high-level competition. She was fortunate that soccer had already begun to take off in the San Diego area, and there were excellent all-girl teams she could join. "Many of the other national team players started off playing on boys teams," she observes. "It's a good option, but not your only option."

After making the Mission Viejo High girls varsity as a freshman in 1986, Julie's game really blossomed. She combined quickness and stamina with a remarkable ability to see the field, and she could think two passes ahead—a rare quality for a player her age. In her sophomore year,

Julie is one of soccer's true "take-charge" players. She agreed to endorse Reebok's new soccer ball only if she could see for herself that no child labor went into making it.

Julie combines amazing stamina with great timing and athletic ability. She played for the national team while still in high school.

she was voted the top player in all of Southern California, and in her junior and senior seasons she was honored as a high school All-American. In 1989, the *Los Angeles Times* named her "Soccer Player of the Decade."

Awards and honors were nice, but Julie had no idea how she would do against better players. She got her first hint when, just before her 17th birthday, she was among five teenagers selected to join the women's national team. The game at that level was much faster, but Julie held her own. She played one game and recorded an assist.

Julie returned to Mission Viejo for her senior season and began sorting through the scholarship offers pouring in from around the country. Ever since the fourth grade Julie had dreamed about attending Stanford University in Northern California—it combined great athletic programs with world-class academics. When the offer from coach Berhane Andeburhan came, she grabbed it.

Julie hit the ground running at Stanford, earning Freshman of the Year honors from *Soccer America*, and being named Player of the Year by that publication as a junior. She led the Cardinal to NCAA Tournament berths all four years, and was an All-American each season. In 1991, Julie set her sights on the big prize: the first Women's World Championship.

Getting Personal

Julie was born on January 23, 1971, in San Diego, California...Julie was an accomplished volleyball player as a kid...In college, she was named Stanford's Outstanding Freshman, Sophomore and Junior Athlete...She finished her college career with 52 goals and 36 assists...At Stanford, Julie earned a degree in Biology...After graduation, she played for the Sacramento Storm, leading the team to the California State Amateur title in 1993, '95 & '97...In 1994, Julie played professionally in Sweden, teaming with Michelle Akers and Kris Lilly on Tyreso Football Club...The media scrutiny following Team USA's gold medal at the 1996 Olympics has changed Julie's life forever. "I think that sometimes, yes, the media does go too far," she says. "But that's their job, to cover the athletes. For women's soccer, it's a welcome change."

She had emerged as one of the top players in the world at that point, and the national team needed her skills in the middle if it expected to get past the semifinals. Julie joined the team for 24 games and started in each, scoring five goals and setting up 10 more. It was a huge commitment that took her away from school for long periods of time. Luckily, her professors kept her from falling behind in her studies. "They were great about faxing me exams and getting my assignments to me overseas," Julie remembers. "It was amazing to get four years of superb education and the awesome athletic program they have there."

Julie played every minute of every game during the World Championships, functioning as an attacking midfielder. She often "quarterbacked" the offense and was a major reason Team USA ended up winning the tournament. Over the next five seasons, Julie became the national team's leader, starting 81 of 82 games through 1997. During that stretch the team lost just seven times when she was on the field.

By the 1996 Olympics, Julie had become more defensive-minded, though her skills as an attacker continued to come into play. In fact, she initiated the sequence that led to Shannon MacMillan's sudden-death goal versus Norway, which catapulted the team into the gold medal final against China.

Off the field, Julie has made a career of thinking ahead and is highly focused on the future. She had a blast at World Cup '99, and plans to stay

Career *Highlights*

Year	Team	Achievement
1987	Mission Viejo	High School All-American
1988	Mission Viejo	High School All-American
1989	Mission Viejo	Southern California Player of the Decade
1989–1992	Stanford	First-Team All-American
1989	Stanford	Soccer America Freshman of the Year
1991	Stanford	Soccer America Player of the Year
1991	Team USA	FIFA World Champion
1996	Team USA	Olympic Gold Medalist
1997	Team USA	FIFA Fair Play Award Winner
1998	Team USA	Goodwill Games Gold Medalist
1998	Team USA	First Career Hat Trick
1999	Team USA	World Cup Champion

active as a player at least through the year 2000. As for the future of soccer, Julie believes that it is bright—especially in America, where high school stars are moving into great college programs and top college players keep feeding into the national squad.

As a key figure in this process, Julie feels responsible for how it changes the "big picture" of soccer. With greater popularity comes an intensified demand for quality equipment. The competition this creates among the world's soccer suppliers has led some manufacturers—most notably in the country of Pakistan—to hire young children to produce their soccer balls. They work long hours for low wages, and the conditions are appalling. Because Julie has traveled the world and seen firsthand how soccer touches so many lives, the thought of children enslaved in the production of the equipment she uses is unacceptable. "It just makes me crazy when a great athlete is asked about the manufacturing of a product he endorses, and he says, 'I don't know anything about that,'" she says.

That is why, when Julie was approached by Reebok to endorse its new line of soccer balls in 1997, she demanded that she first visit the factory where the balls would be made. While the national team was playing in Australia, she hopped a plane to Singapore, connected with a flight headed for Karachi, Pakistan, and then made her way to the village of Sialkot,

Julie blows past Danish defender Kamma Flaeng, who hangs on for dear life. Julie is one of Team USA's most dangerous open-field performers.

where Reebok had set up its plant. Satisfied that no children were sewing her name on the balls, she returned to the team.

Why make the effort? Why not trust the public relations people when they tell you not to worry? It all comes back to responsibility. "I wanted to see with my own eyes how the balls are made, rather than hearing about it from a million miles away," Julie explains. "Being an athlete is a great life. It was an easy decision."

"I'm an introvert, but I'm comfortable expressing myself through soccer. It has everything—fear, frustration, elation. It's the cornerstone of my identity."

Mia Hamm

When Mia Hamm was five years old, her mother decided to enroll her in ballet school. Mia refused, saying she wanted to play for the local Pee Wee soccer team instead. Had Stephanie Hamm put her foot down and stuffed her daughter into a tutu, the course of women's soccer might have been changed forever. Luckily, Mia was allowed to follow her own path.

Perhaps Stephanie—a former ballet dancer—gave in because she wanted to encourage Mia's independence. She was a painfully shy little girl who preferred to blend into the background rather than stand out in a crowd. Normally, this does not pose much of a problem. But Mia's father was a fighter pilot in the Air Force, and every few years the family had to pick up and move to a new base. This meant Mia had to make a whole new group of friends just when she was getting comfortable with the ones she already had. Over the years, the Hamms lived in Alabama, Texas, Virginia and Italy.

Mia felt most comfortable doing the thing she loved: playing soccer. She spent a good portion of her early life sitting on the sidelines, watching her older brothers and sisters play; her dad was a coach and a referee. By the time Mia decided to get in the game, she had absorbed a lot of soccer. She usually played on mixed-sex teams, and she was almost always the best player. She could kick the ball with great power and accuracy, but she also could put a soft pass right on a teammate's foot. She was fast in the open field, quick and creative in a crowd, and had great anticipation and instincts.

When Mia Hamm began playing for the women's national team, crowds sometimes numbered in the hundreds. Today she hears it from thousands of fans, as women's soccer has become a big-time spectator sport.

Mia is a scoring threat from any place on the field. From the right wing, she can shoot, pass or veer into the middle and go right down the throat of the defense.

By the time she reached her teens, Mia had a very mature game. While the family was living in Wichita Falls, Texas, she played for Notre Dame High School. That is where John Cossaboon, who coached an Olympic development team, spotted the 14-year-old phenomenon in 1986. He invited her to play on his team, and she got even better. In 1987, at the U.S. Soccer Federation tournament, Mia got an opportunity to work with Anson Dorrance, coach of the women's national squad. She felt a little lost at times, and the conditioning practically killed her, but she left the tournament knowing she could compete with the country's best players. Dorrance agreed, and later that year she became the youngest member of the team at 15. Mia played in seven games, averaging about 50 minutes per contest.

Over the next two years, Mia played high school ball and also made several appearances for the national team. In the fall of 1989, she joined Coach Dorrance as a freshman at the University of North Carolina, and promptly helped the Tar Heels win the national championship. The following fall, Carolina repeated as national champion. Mia earned All-America honors and led the nation in scoring with 24 goals and 19 assists.

In 1991, Mia made a big decision. She decided to sit out the college season to prepare for the first FIFA Women's World Championships in China. It was her fifth year with the national squad, yet at 19 she was still its youngest member. In the tournament's first match, against Sweden, Mia was pressed into service as an outside midfielder—a position that was completely unfamiliar to her. "I just didn't want to make a mistake," she admits, but adds that the player she was guarding "took me to school." Any mistakes she made were forgiven, however, when she banged home the game-winning goal. Mia scored again in the next game, and played brilliantly the rest of the way, as the United States surged to victory.

Mia returned to UNC, and carved out a special place for herself

Getting Personal

Mia was born on March 17, 1972 in Selma, Alabama...She has two brothers and three sisters. Her brother Garrett died from a rare blood disorder in April of 1996...Mia's given name is Mariel Margaret...According to Mia, she fell in love with soccer because "I could run fast and jump high and kick the ball as hard as I could, and all these great things— and it was actually encouraged."...Mia always ties her right shoe before her left...She graduated as Carolina's all-time leading scorer with 103 goals and 72 assists...Mia graduated from college with a degree in Political Science...During the first Women's World Cup in 1995, Mia played goalie for several minutes after Briana Scurry was ejected in a match against Denmark...She is married to Christian Corry, a Marine Corps pilot...After her soccer days are over, she might give the LPGA Tour a try.

in college soccer. She was not only the top player in the country, but possibly the best player anyone had ever seen. The confidence and experience she had gained in China made her a star of unprecedented magnitude. Mia was a nightmare to contain. She had explosive speed, but could also stop on a dime and then change direction.

The Tar Heels won the national championship again in 1992 and 1993, making it four NCAA titles in four years for Mia, who won the Hermann Trophy both seasons. She also led the nation again with 32

Career Highlights

Year	Team	Achievement
1987	Team USA	Youngest Ever National Team Member
1988	Lake Braddock	High School All-American
1989–1990, 1992–1993	Carolina	NCAA Champion
1990, 1992–1993	Carolina	First-Team All-American
1991	Team USA	FIFA World Champion
1992–1993	Carolina	Hermann Trophy Winner
1992–1993	Carolina	Missouri Athletic Club Award
1994	Carolina	Broderick Award Winner
1994	Team USA	Chiquita Cup MVP
1994–1998	Team USA	US Soccer Female Athlete of the Year
1996	Team USA	Olympic Gold Medalist
1997	Team USA	Women's Sports Foundation Athlete of the Year
1998	Team USA	Goodwill Games Gold Medalist & MVP
1999	Team USA	World Cup Champion & All-Star

goals and 33 assists. The accomplishments and honors kept coming after that. In 1994, Mia played brilliantly at the Chiquita Cup, as the U.S. swept past excellent teams from China, Germany and Norway. She also was named U.S. Soccer's Female Athlete of the Year. At the U.S. Women's Cup in 1995, Mia led the team to the championship, sinking Norway with three spectacular goals on long free kicks. In 1996, she led the team in scoring, and gave opponents fits all year long.

By the time the Olympics started, the whole world knew who Mia was—even fans who never watched a soccer game had heard of her. She showed what she was made of in Atlanta when, after spraining her ankle in the first round against Sweden, she bounced back to perform brilliantly for Team USA. In the final against China, more than 75,000 packed the stadium to watch the United States win the gold medal—a far cry from the 500-or-so spectators who used to turn up for their matches when Mia first joined the team.

After the Olympics, Mia's star continued to rise. At the 1997 U.S. Women's Cup, she scored back-to-back hat tricks in nationally televised games. At the 1998 U.S. Women's Cup, she scored her 100th career goal.

Mia also won MVP honors at the Goodwill Games, and was named Outstanding Female Athlete at the ESPY Awards. In 1999, she tallied her 109th goal to become the all-time leading scorer in women's soccer. And at World Cup '99 Mia blasted two game-winning goals. Her top moment of 1999? Making a Gatorade commercial with Michael Jordan, in which she gets to throw him to the mat during a martial arts encounter. As Mia would be the first to say, it doesn't get any better than that!

Mia celebrates another goal. Even when held scoreless, she is usually the key to Team USA's high-powered offense.

"I am always fighting. I never get down. I'm never negative. Nothing bothers me. I just do what I have to do to get the job done."

Kristine Lilly

No one wants the tag of "Tag-Along Sister." But like it or not, that is what Kristine Lilly was when she was a kid. Her older brother, Scott, played every sport under the sun, and Kris was usually there, either watching or playing with Scott and his friends. Her favorite sports were baseball and basketball, but her best sport was soccer. At the age of six, she easily made the boys' team near her home in Queens, New York. Although she might have preferred playing with other girls, to this day, Kris believes that being the lone girl on the squad was a good thing. "It made a big difference for me," she maintains. "It contributed to my aggressiveness, and it gave me an advantage when I started playing with girls in high school."

Did it ever! By the time she was in high school, the Lilly family had moved north to soccer-mad Wilton, Connecticut. Needless to say, Kris felt right at home. And the coach at Wilton High was thrilled to have her. Even as a 14-year-old freshman, she was the most gifted player on the field. Kris was more than talented—she was a tireless and enthusiastic team leader. No one worked harder in practice and no one did more things to win during games.

In her freshman year, Wilton won the 1985 state championship. During her sophomore year, she received an invitation to play on the national 19-and-under team, which was quite an honor for a player so young. Kris was shocked. "I almost turned it down," she says. "I had just turned 15, but my parents said it would only hurt me if I didn't go."

The road to Olympic gold was a long one for Kris, who first made headlines as a high school star during the mid-1980s.

Kris has appeared in more international games than any player in history. With her experience has come supreme confidence and invaluable leadership.

While playing for the national squad, Kris caught the eye of Anson Dorrance, the legendary coach of the University of North Carolina. When it came time for her to choose which college she would attend, he offered her a scholarship. Carolina had a great team and excellent academics; Kris leaped at the opportunity. Dorrance loved her commitment and work ethic, once saying Kris played with "every cell of her body."

The 5' 4" dynamo blossomed at Carolina, becoming one of the most lethal scorers in the history of women's soccer. During her four years at UNC, the Tar Heels posted a record of 93-1-1 and captured four national championships. Kris was selected as a first-team All-American four times, and earned Most Valuable Offensive Player recognition at the NCAA Championships both as a freshman and sophomore. She finished her collegiate career with 78 goals and 41 assists.

During this period, Kris also had made quite a name for herself on the international scene. In 1991 she played in every game of the first FIFA

Women's World Championship, as Team USA surged to a historic victory in China. Kris says there is one reason above all others that she will never forget that moment. "At the world championships after we won, I looked into the stands and saw my dad," she recalls. "Just to see how happy he was will be forever in my mind."

After that Kris became the workhorse of the national team, averaging better than a point a game and appearing in more international matches than any other player in the world. In 1993, she was named U.S. Soccer's Female Athlete of the Year. At the 1995 Women's World Championship she tied for the team lead with three goals. And by the time the 1996 Olympics rolled around, Kris was hands-down the best flank midfielder in the world. In Atlanta, she played every minute of every game, as Team USA captured the gold medal.

Kris represents the new breed of player in women's soccer. She does not just *play* the game, she lives it, breathes it, eats it and sleeps it. After she graduated from college, she needed to play a lot more than the 20-or-so games a year on the national team's

Getting Personal

Kris was born on July 22, 1971 in New York City...While she feels that competing in male leagues as a youngster helped her a great deal, she doesn't believe that doing so is right for everyone. "If girls are playing with boys and can do it, let them play," she says...She was the first college player to earn first-team All-America honors in each of her four varsity seasons...Kris was awarded the 1991 Hermann Trophy as the country's top female soccer player...In 1994, she had her number 15 retired by UNC...Kris graduated with a degree in Radio, Television, and Motion Picture Production...The only concession she asked the Washington Warthogs to make when she joined the team was that they find her a separate area to shower and change. Playing with the boys is one thing—dressing with them is something else...Although Kris gets far less recognition than Mia Hamm and Michelle Akers, her teammates know what an incredible job she does. "She's someone I want to be like," says Akers. "She's probably the best all-around player on our team, and she plays one of the hardest positions. In a word, she's awesome."

Career *Highlights*

Year	Team	Achievement
1985–1986, 1988	Wilton High	Connecticut State Champion
1989–1992	North Carolina	First-Team All-American & All-ACC
1989–1990	North Carolina	MVP of NCAA Tournament
1990–1991	North Carolina	NCAA Player of the Year
1991	Team USA	FIFA World Champion
1991	Team USA	Hermann Trophy Winner
1993	Team USA	US Soccer Female Athlete of the Year
1993	Team USA	US Sportswoman of the Year
1995	Team USA	Top US Scorer at Women's World Cup
1996	Team USA	Olympic Gold Medalist
1998	Team USA	Goodwill Games Gold Medalist
1998	Team USA	Becomes Most-Capped Woman in History
1999	Team USA	World Cup Champion

schedule. That led her to Europe, where she performed alongside Team USA members Michelle Akers, Julie Foudy and Mary Harvey for Sweden's Tyreso club.

In 1995, Kris found herself in a familiar spot. She was the only female player on the Washington Warthogs of the Continental Indoor Soccer League. In fact, she was the only woman playing in the entire league. Kris earned a spot on the team thanks to the husband of Carin Gabarra, who retired from the national team in 1998. Her husband, Jim, was the Warthog coach. Why go back to playing with the boys when you are one of the greatest players in the history of women's soccer? As always, Kris was being pragmatic. "A lot of people on the national team either compete for their colleges or coach in the fall, but I didn't really have anyone to work-out with," she says of her decision. "The indoor game is so fast, it helps my quickness, mentally and physically, and forces me to make earlier decisions when I have the ball. Guys are always a step ahead in quickness and strength."

She fails to mention, of course, that by season's end she had established herself as one of the better players in the CISL. In the meantime, Kris

Having a veteran like Kris "running the show" has allowed younger players such as Mia Hamm (right) to flourish.

continues to plug away for the national team. In 1997, she started every one of the team's 18 international matches and played more minutes than anyone else. She has also opened her own soccer academy in Wilton.

In 1998 and 1999, Kris proved to be Team USA's smartest and most durable player. The woman who has played more games than anyone in history played her best in the biggest game of her career. Against China in the final of World Cup '99, Kris deflected a certain goal to preserve a tie, then scored during the ensuing shootout to seal Team USA's victory. No one who knows her would have expected anything less.

ON HER MIND

"I don't feel any pressure. If I just play my game, I know something is going to happen."

Shannon MacMillan

What makes a true champion? It is a simple enough question, but the answer can be quite complex. It is more than winning, certainly. More, even, than making the big plays in the big games. Indeed, to reach the the absolute heights in sports, you have to have experienced the depths. Shannon MacMillan knows all about that. A few years ago she was written off by the soccer community, only to scratch and claw her way back into the spotlight. And when Shannon finally got a shot at greatness, she scored what many rate as the most important goal in the history of U.S. soccer.

Her odyssey began in 1980, after the MacMillan family moved from Long Island to Southern California. A few of the neighborhood kids persuaded five-year-old Shannon to join a local soccer league. "I instantly loved it," she recalls. "I picked it up pretty fast, but I wasn't the best."

Though new to soccer, Shannon displayed a real feel for the game. She could sense opportunities developing and usually found herself in the right place at the right time. Fast and aggressive, Shannon would go all-out for the goal whenever she got the ball. She continued to develop these skills right through grade school and junior high, and by the time she was in high school she was one of the best players in the area.

Shannon could not get enough of soccer. She was the star of the San Pasqual High team, earning league MVP recognition three times and being named the top schoolgirl player in the county as a sophomore, junior and senior. In her final year she scored a school-record 41 goals. Meanwhile, Shannon was also playing for a local adult team called the La

Shannon rebounded from a heartbreaking injury to become a heart-stopping performer.

Shannon spots an open teammate. Her passing touch is as good as her scoring ability.

Jolla Nomads. The Nomads won championships in 1991 and 1992, with Shannon leading the charge.

When it came time to think about college, a lot of coaches felt Shannon was too "fragile" for Division I play. With her choices limited, she decided to attend the University of Portland, in Oregon. She looked forward to teaming with Tiffeny Milbrett, the Pilots' best player. Shannon's first year was a great one, as she netted 19 goals and collected 10 assists—tops among all college freshmen. As a sophomore, she led the nation in scoring and made All-American. She was even better in her junior year—so good, in fact, that there were whispers that the team might even have a shot at the national championship.

But just when all those coaches who had questioned Shannon's durability were ready to eat their words, it suddenly looked as if they might be right. With the NCAA Tournament just a few weeks away, Shannon broke her left foot. She played two games before the pain became unbearable; amazingly, she scored four goals). Doctors inserted a pin in her foot and Shannon was back in the lineup in time for the tournament. She led Portland all the way to the semifinals before Notre Dame eliminated the Pilots with a 1-0 victory.

In 1995, Shannon went out for the national team, but could not make it through tryouts because of recurring pain in her foot. She took some time off, returned to school, and started what she hoped would be a championship senior season. But in the opener against Oregon State, the always aggressive Shannon collided with the goaltender. Her teammates watched in horror as she clutched her left knee and writhed in pain. They knew Shannon was not one of those players who lies on the ground and pretends to be hurt just to catch her breath. She was in trouble. Shannon was taken to the bench, where her knee swelled up like a balloon. The Portland trainer feared the knee was torn to shreds, but that evening it was determined that she had only strained the ligaments. With a little rest and rehabilitation, she would be back on the field in no time.

With the words of her detractors no doubt echoing in her head, Shannon showed up for the team's game against the University of Washington—the very next day. She even managed to talk her way into the lineup for 20 minutes!

Basically, there was no way Shannon was going to spend her senior year recuperating. Playing in pain all season long, Shannon had 23 goals and 16 assists for a career-high 62 points. She was showered with awards after the season, including the coveted Hermann Trophy as the nation's top player.

Shannon immediately started searching for new challenges. She wanted to win a gold medal at the 1996 Olympics, and decided to try out for

Getting Personal

Shannon was born on October 7, 1974, in Syosset, New York...A good student, she was once named to the San Diego Union-Tribune's All-Academic Team...She led the La Jolla Nomads all the way to the national club soccer finals in 1991...In 1993, Shannon was a member of the national Under-20 team that won the International Women's Tournament in France...She was twice voted the University of Portland's Female Athlete of the Year...While in college, Shannon's favorite soccer player was Kristine Lilly—now one of her teammates...When Shannon wants to relax she takes a ride on her wave runner...Her rise to fame in the Olympics may not have been a coincidence. "As a kid, I was always watching the Olympics," she recalls. "Watching the emotion the athletes went through...I just wanted to feel that."...She received the "key to the city" of Escondido after winning the Olympics.

Career Highlights

Year	Team	Achievement
1988–1991	San Pasqual HS	CIF Champion
1991–1992	La Jolla	California Club Champion
1993	Portland	NCAA Scoring Champion
1993–1995	Portland	First-Team All-American
1995	Portland	Soccer America Player of the Year
1995	Portland	Missouri Athletic Club Award Winner
1995	Portland	Hermann Trophy Winner
1996	Team USA	Olympic Gold Medalist
1998	Team USA	Goodwill Games Gold Medalist
1999	Team USA	World Cup Champion

the national team again. Shannon quickly discovered that being the reigning queen of college soccer held little sway with coach Tony DiCicco. She was a forward trying to crack a lineup deep at that position. She would have to outplay Mia Hamm, Carin Gabarra, Michelle Akers and Tiffeny Milbrett—each of whom ranked among the top offensive players in the world. Shannon did well, but when DiCicco had to make his final cuts he decided to go with experience. When he told her, she went ballistic. "I stormed out of there," Shannon remembers. "I thought my world had ended."

Just when things looked their darkest, however, a little luck finally came Shannon's way. A few weeks later, nine members of the national team banded together in protest of a bonus system that would only compensate the players if they won the gold medal in Atlanta. Coach DiCicco tracked down Shannon and invited her to join the team, with one catch: she would have to be a halfback, a position she had never played before. Shannon knew an opportunity when she saw one, and agreed to his terms. Although the protesting players returned, Shannon nailed down a spot on the team by adjusting quickly to the halfback role. In the months leading up to the Olympics, she established herself as one of Team USA's most valuable all-around players.

As the Olympics began, Shannon logged important minutes in the first three games, which the U.S. won with relative ease. In the semifinals against Norway, with the score knotted 1-1, she was sent into the game to start the sudden-death overtime period. Four minutes later, she watched a play develop from her halfback slot and suddenly her scorer's mentality kicked in. She streaked toward the goal just in time to redirect a ball by Julie Foudy past the goaltender and into the net. A wild celebration followed, with Shannon right in the middle. The next day, while everyone was still buzzing about her heroics, Shannon came through

again with the opening goal in a 2-1 win over China, and then kept the pressure on all game long. At this point, even her sternest doubters had to shake their heads and smile. In the end, the girl who was too small, too fragile, and too inexperienced had been too stubborn to give up.

And she had the gold medal to prove it.

Shannon's second chance to make the national team proved to be a golden opportunity.

ON HER MIND

"I don't ever expect to win—
I know the hard work and
dedication it takes to get there."

Carla Overbeck

peed and agility aren't always the main ingredients in the makeup of a star athlete. Sometimes intelligence and passion can get you just as far. Take sweeper Carla Overbeck, captain of the U.S. team that won gold at the 1996 Olympics and took the World Cup in 1999. "I'm really too slow, and I don't have that many moves, either," she says. What Carla does have is an intense desire to achieve and succeed. Plus, she adores the game she plays.

Carla's love affair with soccer began after her family moved to Dallas. She started playing at age five and improved steadily until, at the age of 11, she made a 14-and-under team that played games all over the state. By the time Carla reached high school, she was so involved in club soccer that she did not even bother to go out for the Richardson High team, playing volleyball and basketball instead.

It was during a club game that Carla was spotted by University of North Carolina coach Anson Dorrance, who was scouting the area for players. He loved Carla's leadership skills and her remarkable presence of mind. She seemed to know how each play would develop, where she should be, and

Being a mother and an international soccer star is not enough for Carla. She is always looking for new projects and challenges.

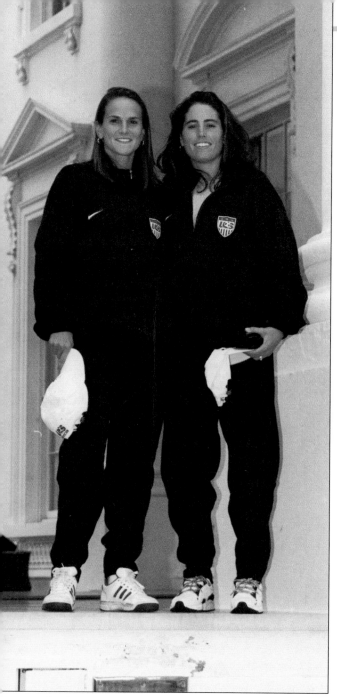

*Carla and Julie Foudy at the White House.
The team was invited by President Clinton
after the Olympics.*

how to position her teammates. Every coach loves to have a "second coach" on the field, and Dorrance felt Carla could fill that roll for the Tar Heels. He offered her a scholarship and the rest, as they say, is history.

North Carolina won four straight NCAA Championships while Carla was there. She made *Soccer America's* All-Freshman team in 1987 and was a First-Team All-American every year after that. She learned a lot from coach Dorrance, and credits him with turning her into one of the top players in the world. "He's very good at recognizing talent," Carla says. "And he's the reason I'm so competitive."

That competitiveness earned Carla a spot on the national team in 1988, and she quickly established herself as the leader of a young and inexperienced team.

By 1991, the players on the national squad had grown together and become a factor in international soccer. That year they won the FIFA Women's World Championship. The secret of their success was a defense that allowed just five goals in six games, and it was Carla who was the focal point of the back line. In 1993, the U.S. women won the CONCACAF Championship in New York. And in August of the same year Carla launched one of the most amazing endurance streaks in the annals of women's soccer. Beginning with a game against New Zealand, she started and finished 39 consecutive international games without leaving the field once for a rest. The incredible run spanned 3,482 minutes and 18 different opponents. More than 80 percent of those matches resulted in victories for the Americans. Why kill yourself staying on the field, even when the team is way ahead? "I just love to play," Carla smiles.

Ironically, one of her most cherished victories came when she was standing on the sidelines. In 1994, while working as an assistant coach for Duke University, she faced her mentor, Coach Dorrance, for the first time. As usual, the Tar Heels were looking invincible. In fact, Carolina came into the game

Getting Personal

Carla was born on May 9, 1968, in Pasadena, California...The family moved to Dallas, Texas, a few years later...Carla credits her parents for helping her progress so quickly. "They were great," she says. "They let me do what I wanted. They didn't push me. Soccer is a game where you have to be mentally strong and psychologically tough. Kids have to grow into it."...Although she did not play soccer for Richardson High School, Carla gained a reputation as one of the top schoolgirl sweepers in the country...She graduated from UNC with a degree in Psychology...Carla was a finalist for the 1995 Women's Sports Foundation Athlete of the Year, along with Bonnie Blair, Steffi Graf, Picabo Street and Rebecca Lobo...She is called the "Cal Ripken" of women's soccer for her amazing endurance...Carla married Greg Overbeck in December of 1992. He is part owner of several restaurants in the Chapel Hill-Durham-Raleigh area...Carla stays in shape between national team training camps by playing for a local co-ed team in Dallas. "I enjoy the competition provided by the guys because they are often faster and stronger than the women," she says...Carla knows part of being a leader is keeping your teammates loose. "She can be funny, crazy and a little bit nuts at times," says Michelle Akers. "Many times, her humor has broken the tedium of the training routine and given the team a lift."

Career Highlights

Year	Team	Achievement
1987	North Carolina	NCAA Champion
1988	North Carolina	First-Team All-American & NCAA Champion
1989	North Carolina	First-Team All-American & NCAA Champion
1990	North Carolina	First-Team All-American & NCAA Champion
1991	Team USA	FIFA World Champion
1996	Team USA	Named Team Captain
1996	Team USA	Olympic Gold Medalist
1998	Team USA	Goodwill Games Gold Medalist
1999	Team USA	World Cup All-Star
1999	Team USA	World Cup Champion

without having lost in 101 games, which still stands as the longest unbeaten streak in the history of college or professional sports. Carla got her players fired up, spotted some minor flaws in the Tar Heel scheme, and helped coach them to a shocking 2-1 victory. The pinnacle of her career came a couple of years later, when Team USA rolled into Atlanta for the 1996 Olympics—and rolled over the competition to win the gold medal.

At 28, she had nothing left to prove in soccer, so she and her husband, Greg, began planning for the next big event: the birth of their first child. On August 14, 1997, Jackson Overbeck arrived and changed their lives forever. But as much as Carla enjoys motherhood, she is also itching to return to the soccer field. That is nothing new. "After the first world championship, I was going to retire," she laughs. "Then the 1995 World Championships came up, then the Olympics, and then the 1999 World Cup was awarded to the United States."

Carla not only played in World Cup '99, she was named to the tournament All-Star squad. Now is it finally time to retire? No way! Her trophy case still has room for one more medal—hopefully another gold one. Look for Carla at the 2000 Olympics.

Carla takes charge from the sweeper position

"Never did I think that I would have an Olympic gold medal over my fireplace."

Briana
Scurry

T he life of a goalkeeper is often lonely. When play is at the other end of the field, you feel like the only person on the planet. And when the defense collapses and an opponent comes in on goal, there is no one in the world who can help you. Briana Scurry knows all about feelings of isolation. Not only is she goalkeeper of the U.S. women's national team, but she is a black woman competing in a sport dominated by whites.

How does one become a goalie? Briana did not have much choice. She was the only girl on her youth soccer team, and none of the boys wanted to play the position. Briana turned out to be a pretty good goalie, and grew to really like her role. During the winter, she played basketball, and this helped with her jumping, footwork and anticipation. But by the time she reached high school, she had decided to concentrate on soccer. "I liked basketball better than soccer," she explains, "but I would have been a dime-a-dozen basketball player. I knew I could go further as a goalkeeper."

Briana became the top schoolgirl goalie in the U.S. during her four years at Anoka High in suburban Minneapolis, and was recruited by a number of top schools. A good student, she wanted to earn a degree that would help her later in life. Briana decided to attend the University of Massachusetts—it had an excellent soccer team and a strong academic reputation. There she fashioned a remarkable college career. With Briana in the net, UMass went 48-13-4. She posted 37 shutouts and averaged

Briana Scurry blocks a penalty shootout kick by China's Ying Liu during overtime of the Women's World Cup Final.

As soon as Briana controls the ball, she begins thinking like an offensive player, always looking to start the attack.

one goal allowed for every two games she played! In 1993, Briana led the Minutewomen to the semifinals of the NCAA tournament. Her goals-against average in her senior season was third best in the nation.

Looking back, Briana actually feels she could have done even better. A goalie has a unique view of the field, and can often see scoring threats develop before her teammates. In these instances, talking to the defenders is crucial. Yet Briana was—and in many respects, still is—a "quiet" goalie. "In high school and college, I never spoke to anyone," she explains, "and that's why I was making 20 to 25 saves a game."

What Briana lacked in communication skills, she more than made up for with her incredible focus and concentration. Her trademark "scowl" has unnerved many a shooter. "I've been told that a lot," she laughs. "'Bri, you look like you're gonna *kill* someone!' I've always had a very intense playing style."

That is what impressed Anson Dorrance the first time he saw Briana, in 1992. Two years later he invited her to join the national team. Adjusting to life at the soccer world's highest level was a bit of a challenge. "Like other girls, I'd dreamed about how cool it would be to play with them," recalls Briana. "Back home in Minnesota, my nephew and I stood in line to have a poster signed by Michelle Akers, and now I'm on the same team with her."

Briana began as a backup to Sue Harvey, and expected to see limited action. But when Sue injured her back, Briana was pressed into service. Her first test was in the Chiquita Cup, and she passed with flying colors. She shutout Portugal to begin the tournament and provided a rock-solid last line of defense as the team made it all the way to the final against Norway. Briana was superb in that game, and the U.S. won, 4-1. She was named MVP.

Getting Personal

Briana was born on September 7, 1971, in Minneapolis, Minnesota...She is the youngest of nine children...The family moved to the suburb of Dayton when she was five...Briana first encountered racism on the soccer field in high school. When things got really tough, Briana was always able to call on her brothers and sisters....Though she stands just 5-8, Briana has long arms and tremendous leaping ability...How does she feel about playing such a dangerous position? "Being a goalkeeper excites me as much as it scares me," she says. "On a big save, when you're almost kicked, it's a rush. On a low ball in front, you risk your face and neck."...Briana played three games as forward for UMass in 1992...She graduated from college in the spring of 1995 with a degree in political science...Briana made her debut with the U.S. team March 16, 1994, against Portugal. She recorded a 5-0 shutout...Briana plans on owning her own business, and hopes to be financially independent by the time she turns 30...Briana punts the ball differently than most goalkeepers. She holds the ball with her right hand, even though she kicks with her right foot...Briana turned in seven shutouts in 1997 and a record 12 shutouts in 1998...She earned All-Star recognition for her play in World Cup '99.

Career Highlights

Year	Team	Achievement
1989	Anoka High	High School All-American
1989	Anoka High	Minnesota Female Athlete of the Year
1993	UMass	National Goalkeeper of the Year
1993	UMass	Atlantic 10 Champion & Second-Team All-American
1994	Team USA	Chiquita Cup MVP
1996	Team USA	Olympic Gold Medalist
1998	Team USA	Goodwill Games Gold Medalist
1999	Team USA	World Cup Champion

That performance earned her more playing time in 1995, and she responded beautifully. The national team went 11-2-2 with Briana in goal, and each of her 11 victories was a shutout. The only smudge on her record was a goal she allowed against Norway in a 1-0 loss. It cost her team the 1995 World Championship.

That disappointment was erased a year later in Atlanta. Briana was brilliant during the 1996 Olympics, allowing just two goals in four matches as the U.S. team advanced to the final. Against China, she played well in a 2-1 victory that brought Briana and her teammates the gold medal. After the celebrating was over, someone reminded Briana of a boast she had made. Prior to the game she had told a reporter that she would run naked through the streets if the team won. Briana kept her word, though she waited until two in the morning, when the streets of Athens, Georgia, were empty and all the television crews had disappeared. All she had on was her gold medal. "I was very naked," she laughs.

Briana hopes to stay in the game long after her playing days and make soccer more accessible to kids like herself. She describes the sport as being "non-colorful" in this country, with African Americans making up just 3% of participants in the U.S. "Perhaps seeing me on TV or hearing me speak will help them to realize that soccer is a sport they, too, can play," she says. "The opportunities now for blacks are just phenomenal!"

We Win!

Briana Scurry kept her clothes on for the 1999 Women's World Cup. As a matter of fact, she turned out to be the key player of the tournament. In each of the final two games her sparkling play spelled the difference between defeat and victory for Team USA, which traveled a long and unexpectedly bumpy road to the title.

Heading into the World Cup, many assumed that victory for the American women was all but guaranteed. But Tony DiCicco knew Team USA would have a fight on its hands. After gold-medal performances at the 1998 Goodwill Games and 1998 U.S. Women's Cup, the team suffered two distressing blows.

First, charges were leveled at UNC's Anson Dorrance by some of his former players, who claimed that he had engaged in inappropriate behavior. Most of the Team USA players came to Dorrance's defense, but some did not. This created fractures in the team at a most inopportune time. Next, there was an embarrassing loss to China in the finals of the Algarve Cup.

Coach DiCicco used this defeat as a wakeup call, reminding his players that they were not invincible, and that much hard work still lay ahead. The team was focused and sharp by the time World Cup '99 began, but DiCicco had another concern. How would the players react to the crush of publicity, the constant roar of 50,000 to 75,000 crazed fans, and the prospect of playing each of their games on national television?

Against first-round opponents Denmark and Nigeria, there were some anxious moments in the early going, but the team was able to relax and

Brandi Chastain celebrates by taking off her jersey after kicking the game winning overtime penalty shootout kick against China during the Women's World Cup Final

win. Against Germany in the quarterfinals, the team again started slowly and found itself on the short end of a 2-1 halftime score. Fortunately, they tightened their defense and pulled it out with a pair of second-half goals. Having regained its confidence, the team went up against the dangerous Brazilians in the semifinals. Brazil peppered the acrobatic Scurry with shots, but she held firm to secure a 2-0 victory and a berth in the finals against China.

More than 90,000 fans jammed the Rose Bowl in California to watch the World Cup final. It was the largest crowd ever to attend a women's sporting event in the U.S., and 40 million more Americans watched the contest on television. In a thrilling display of skill, stamina, and perseverance, the Chinese and Americans launched attacks and counterattacks on each other, with one terrific offensive move followed by an even better defensive effort. After 90 nail-biting minutes of intense soccer, the teams were deadlocked in a scoreless tie. Two overtime periods proved fruitless, as the players just seemed to get better and the score held at 0-0. Finally, the battle had to be decided with a shootout, soccer's ultimate one-on-one showdown.

China shot first and scored. Then Carla Overbeck responded with a goal of her own. China scored again, but Joy Fawcett tied it up. Next, the powerful Liu Ying blasted a ball that was headed just inside the left post. Scurry sensed this was where Liu was going, and propelled her body through the air. With her arms stretched as far as they would go, she managed to punch the ball out of harm's way.

After Kris Lilly and Mia Hamm traded goals with their Chinese counterparts, Brandi Chastain sent a left-footed laser past Chinese goalie Gao Hong to seal a 5-4 shootout victory. Chastain, nicknamed "Hollywood" by her teammates, dropped to her knees, tore off her shirt, screamed her head off, and then disappeared under a pile of red-white-and-blue jerseys.

One day we all will look back on this game and celebrate it as a turning point in sports. The skill, drama, and emotion of the players captivated the world, and lifted women's soccer onto a higher plane. More importantly, it inspired millions of young girls to get into the game. How many participants in the 2011 World Cup will tell of the time they sat mesmerized as Team USA and China dueled for three magnificent hours? Don't be surprised if the answer is *every single one*.

Brandi Chastain, center, is greeted by teammates Shannon MacMillan (8), Sara Whalen (7) and Kate Sobrero (20) after kicking the game-winning overtime penalty shootout kick

INDEX

PAGE NUMBERS IN ITALICS REFER TO ILLUSTRATIONS.